P9-APT-660

Dear Parent:
Your child's love of reading starts here!

Every child learns to read in a different way and at his or her own speed. Some go back and forth between reading levels and read favorite books again and again. Others read through each level in order. You can help your young reader improve and become more confident by encouraging his or her own interests and abilities. From books your child reads with you to the first books he or she reads alone, there are I Can Read Books for every stage of reading:

SHARED READING
Basic language, word repetition, and whimsical illustrations, ideal for sharing with your emergent reader

BEGINNING READING
Short sentences, familiar words, and simple concepts for children eager to read on their own

READING WITH HELP
Engaging stories, longer sentences, and language play for developing readers

READING ALONE
Complex plots, challenging vocabulary, and high-interest topics for the independent reader

ADVANCED READING
Short paragraphs, chapters, and exciting themes for the perfect bridge to chapter books

I Can Read Books have introduced children to the joy of reading since 1957. Featuring award-winning authors and illustrators and a fabulous cast of beloved characters, I Can Read Books set the standard for beginning readers.

A lifetime of discovery begins with the magical words "I Can Read!"

Visit www.icanread.com for information
on enriching your child's reading experience.

I Can Read!

READING
2
WITH HELP

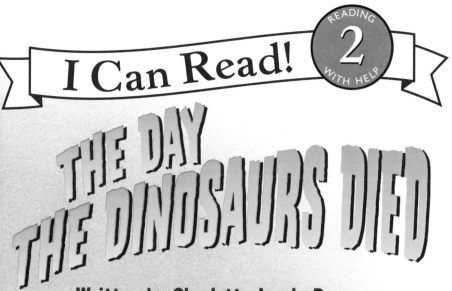

THE DAY THE DINOSAURS DIED

Written by Charlotte Lewis Brown

Illustrated by Phil Wilson

HarperCollins*Publishers*

I wrote this book for Anne
—C.L.B.

For my parents and my high school art teacher,
Bill Applequist, with gratitude
—P.W.

HarperCollins®, 🐾®, and I Can Read Book® are trademarks of HarperCollins Publishers Inc.

Library of Congress Cataloging-in-Publication Data
Brown, Charlotte Lewis.
    The day the dinosaurs died / story by Charlotte Lewis Brown ; pictures by Phil Wilson.— 1st ed.
    p.   cm. — (I can read book)
    ISBN-10: 0-06-000528-9 (trade bdg.) — ISBN-13: 978-0-06-000528-3 (trade bdg.)
    ISBN-10: 0-06-000529-7 (lib. bdg.) — ISBN-13: 978-0-06-000529-0 (lib. bdg.)
    1. Dinosaurs—Extinction—Juvenile literature. 2. Competition (Biology)—Juvenile literature. I. Wilson, Phil. II. Title. III. Series.
QE861.6.E95B76 2006
567.9—dc22   2005015135

1   2   3   4   5   6   7   8   9   10   ❖   First Edition

HOW TO SAY:

Alamosaurus (al-uh-moe-SAWR-us)

Dromaeosaurus (DROH-mee-oh-SAWR-us)

Edmontosaurus (ed-MON-toh-SAWR-us)

Parasaurolophuses (PAR-ah-saw-ROL-oh-fus-es)

Pteranodons (ter-AN-oh-dons)

Triceratops (tri-SER-uh-tops)

Tyrannosaurus rex (tye-RAN-oh-SAWR-us recks)

Long, long ago,
dinosaurs were everywhere.
They hunted by the sea
and high in the hills.
They walked across
dry, sandy deserts.
They ran through
wet, green jungles.
For millions of years,
the dinosaurs ruled the earth.
Now they are all gone.
How did they die?
It may have happened like this. . .

Tyrannosaurus rex roared.

The Dromaeosaurus pack

stopped eating.

They looked up

at Tyrannosaurus rex.

One Dromaeosaurus
grabbed a last bite
of Edmontosaurus meat.
Then the whole pack ran.

Tyrannosaurus rex walked over
to the dead Edmontosaurus,
and he ripped out a large bite.

Tyrannosaurus rex

watched for other dinosaurs

as he ate.

He did not want to share his food.

He looked right and left.

He looked in front and in back.

But he didn't look up at the sky.

He didn't see

the strange new light there.

It looked like a very bright star.

It was not.

It was a giant asteroid.

It was heading toward Earth.

The asteroid grew brighter

as it came closer.

Tyrannosaurus rex

did not notice.

He just kept eating.

Pteranodons flew in circles
high above Tyrannosaurus rex.
They cried out
as the light grew brighter.
Tyrannosaurus rex
did not even look up.
He just kept eating.

Soon the asteroid
blazed brighter
than the sun.

Tyrannosaurus rex looked up at last.

It was too late.

The asteroid burst
into a ball of fire.
It filled the whole sky.
Tyrannosaurus rex
roared one last time.
Then . . .
Kaboom!

The fireball smashed into the ground.

Tyrannosaurus rex died instantly.

The Pteranodons

were blown from the sky.

Their bodies

burned away to nothing.

Everything for miles around
burned up in the explosion.
Dinosaurs, trees, dirt,
and even some stones boiled away.
Huge rocks were thrown
into the sky.

Some rocks flew off into space.
Most rocks fell back to Earth,
burning as they came.

The asteroid blasted a giant hole
in the ground called a crater.
This crater was more than
100 miles wide.
The destruction had just begun.
A wall of fire sped out
from the crater in all directions.

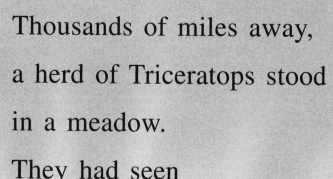

Thousands of miles away,
a herd of Triceratops stood
in a meadow.
They had seen
a bright flash of light.

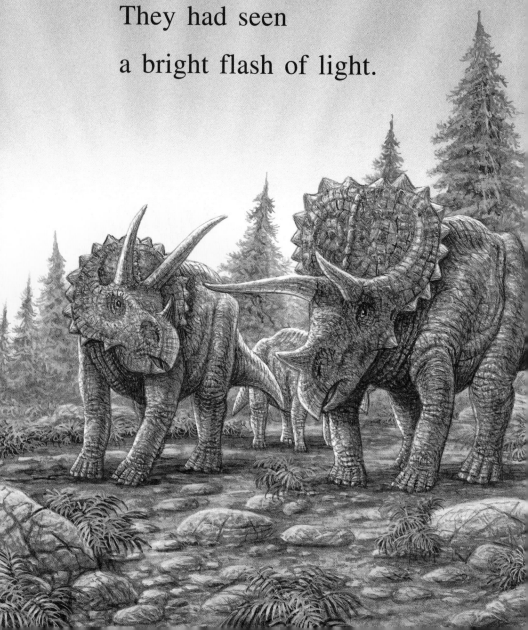

Now everything looked normal.

Still, they sensed danger.

But they didn't know

where—or what—it was.

A large male bellowed
and stomped his foot.
He dared the enemy
to come out and fight.
All of the Triceratops
were scared.

Only Alamosaurus was not scared.
She moved to the next tree
and pulled off a branch to eat.

Suddenly, the sky glowed red.

A blast of wind roared past.

The Triceratops were knocked over.

The trees bent, then broke.

One tree crushed Alamosaurus.

The Triceratops
struggled to their feet and ran.
Burning rocks crashed down
from the sky.
Trees and bushes burst into flames.
One rock struck a Triceratops.
He fell and did not get up.
The rest of the herd ran on.

The fire spread too fast.
Soon the Triceratops
had no place left to run.

Flames closed in from all sides.

Then another roar

rose above the fire.

A wall of muddy water
swept in from the distant sea.
The asteroid had created
a giant tidal wave.

The wave drowned the flames.

But it also drowned the Triceratops.

It left everything buried

under a thick layer of mud.

Around the world, burning rocks
still fell from the sky.
More forest fires blazed.

Thick black smoke filled the sky.

Day turned darker than night.

Many dinosaurs died in the flames.

Others choked on the thick smoke.

Only a few survived that first day.

They hid from the fires

as their world burned.

Weeks passed.

At last the fires died away.
In the far north,
a few Parasaurolophuses
had survived.

They had hidden in a deep cave.

Many had been hurt.

All of them were hungry.

The Parasaurolophuses
limped slowly out of the cave.
The day was dark and cold.
Smoke still hid the sun.
Ashes covered everything.

The other dinosaurs
were now only bones.

The Parasaurolophuses
searched for plants to eat,
but there were none.
All the plants had burned to ashes.
For days they wandered.

Some tried eating ashes.

Some were so hungry they ate dirt.

Nothing helped.

Each day they grew weaker.

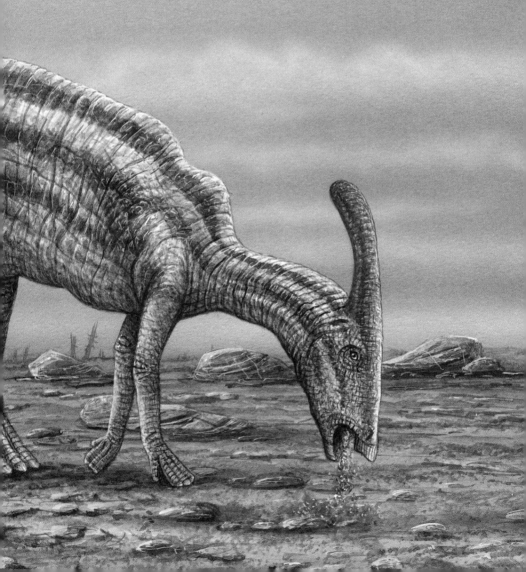

One by one they began to die.

Soon there was only one left.

Then she too starved away.

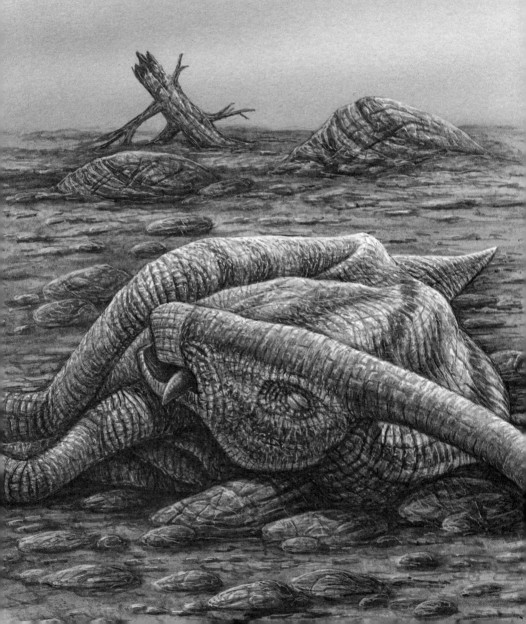

Two small, furry animals sniffed
the last Parasaurolophus.
They were mammals.
They had survived the fire
in their underground tunnels.
The mammals came out
looking for food.
They dug deep under the ashes
and found roots to eat.
Some mammals ate dead dinosaurs.

After many, many months,
the smoke began to clear.
The sun shown again in the sky.
Plants began to grow
from buried seeds.

The mammals had survived.

Now the world was theirs.

Author's Note

The dinosaurs thrived for more than 120 million years. Then they suddenly disappeared about 65 million years ago. Most scientists believe that the dinosaurs died out because a large asteroid or a comet hit Earth. This impact left a crater more than 100 miles wide near the Yucatán Peninsula, in modern Mexico. It also caused earthquakes, giant tidal waves, global forest fires, and other disasters described in this book. While we don't know exactly how all the dinosaurs died, many would have perished in the disasters caused by the impact. The Tyrannosaurus rex in this story was living on an island near where the asteroid (or comet) hit Earth. The Triceratops herd lived more than 1,000 miles to the north, in modern Texas. The Parasaurolophus herd lived in Canada. Although the dinosaurs became extinct, many animals survived the impact, including the ancestors of modern mammals.